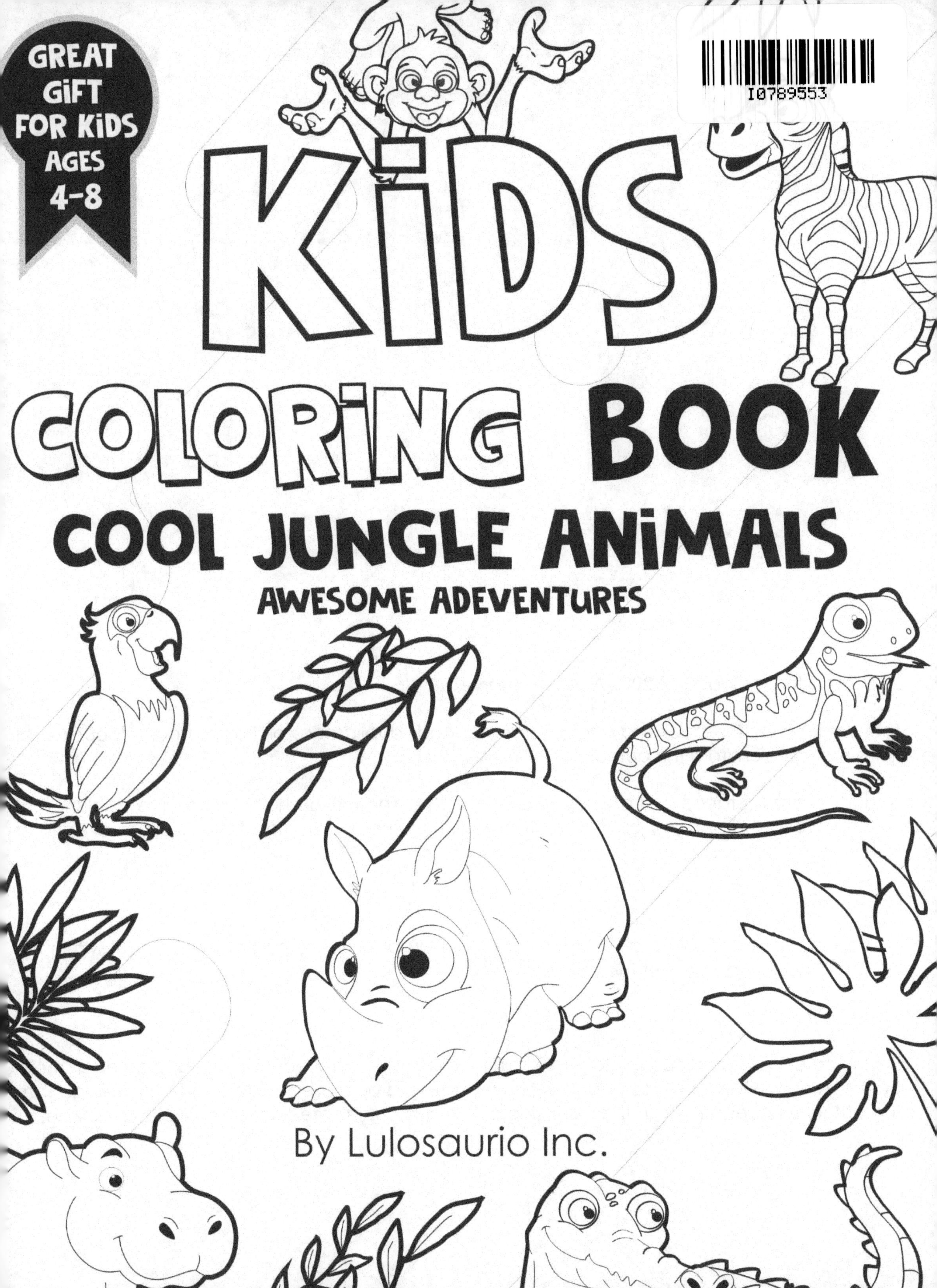

GREAT GIFT FOR KIDS AGES 4-8
KIDS
COLORING BOOK
COOL JUNGLE ANIMALS
AWESOME ADEVENTURES
By Lulosaurio Inc.
I0789553

LuloSaurio Inc. ©Copyright 2020 All rights reserved.

The contents of this book may not be reproduced, duplicated, or transmitted without direct written permission from the author.

Under no circumstances will any legal responsibility or blame be held against the publisher for any reparation, damages, or monetary loss due to the information herein, either directly or indirectly.

Legal Notice:

You cannot amend, distribute, sell, use, quote or paraphrase any part of the content within this book without the consent of the author.

Disclaimer Notice:

Please note the information contained within this document is for educational and entertainment purposes only. No warranties of any kind are expressed or implied. Readers acknowledge that the author is not engaging in the rendering of legal, financial, medical or professional advice.

INTRODUCTION

The jungle animals are incredibly amazing. We selected the most representative ones so that the children could color them and learn curious facts that perhaps they did not know.

At Lulosaurio Inc. we want to pay tribute to so many of these beautiful animals that are even in danger of extinction.

We hope you enjoy every page of this book as much as we do!

We appreciate your reviews in order to get better everyday.

Most of the time my tail is
longer than my body

I love to eat
plants

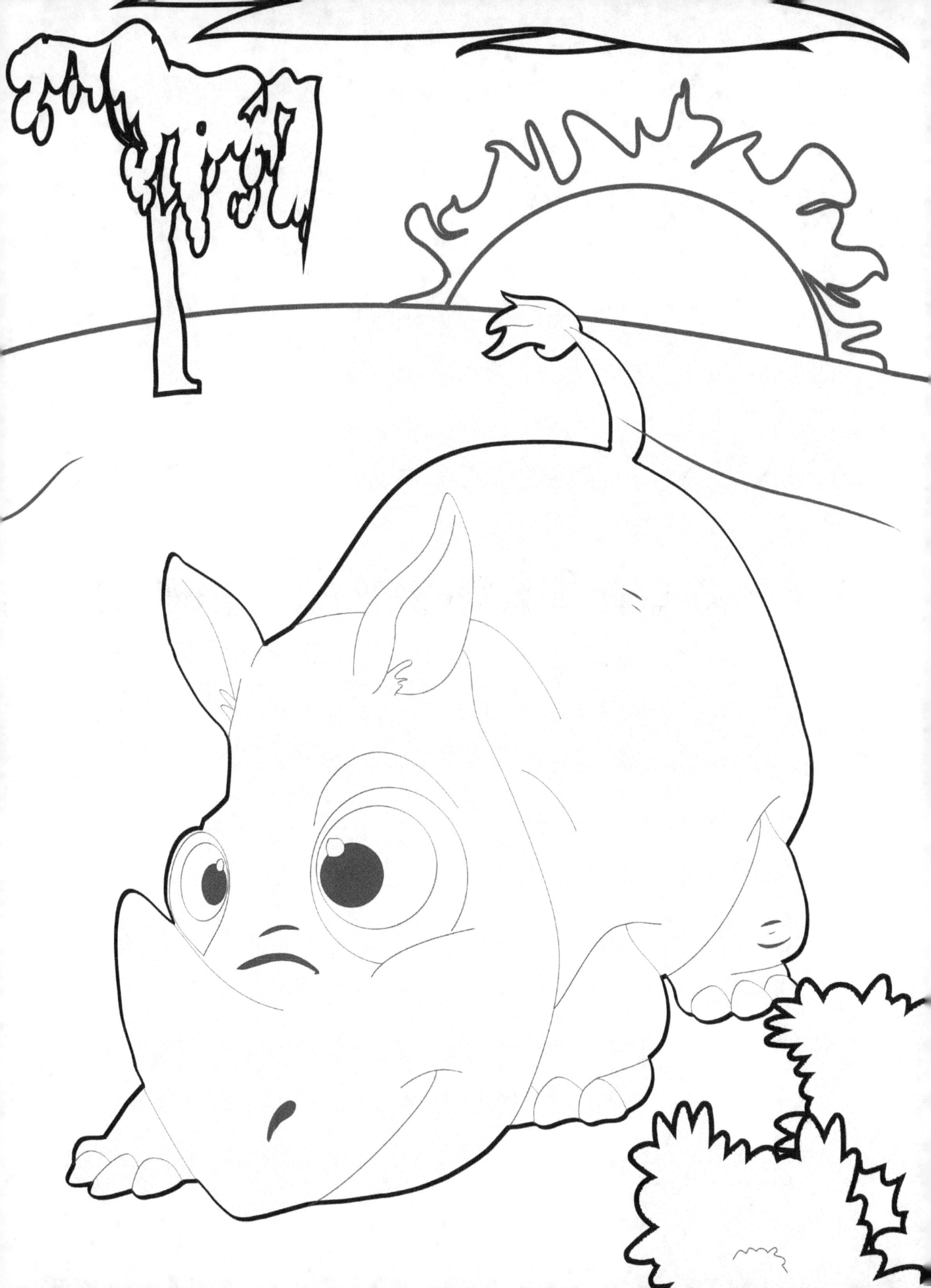

We don't know to swim

My babies are
born underwater

I can see forward and backwards at the

same time

I CAN HOLD MY BREATH
UNDER WATER FOR
TWO DAYS, IF I DON'T
MOVE AT ALL

I am a great
swimmer

I DON'T CLOSE MY EYES EVEN WHEN I SLEEP

I LIKE TO KISS AND HUG

I am black with white stripes

i am the largest parrot

WE ARE AFRAID OF ANTS AND BEES

I use my tail to keep my balance

I am the biggest cat in the world

LIZARD

CROCODILE

Hippopotamus
Rhino

JAGUAR
FROG

Macaw

Chimpanzee

Snake
Tiger

Zebra

Elephant

MONKEY

CHIMPANZEE

Zebra
Giraffe

Gazelle

Chameleon

SNAKE

FROG

Lion

Jaguar

Rhino

Crocodile

I AM VERY FAST
BECAUSE OF THE SHAPE
OF MY LEGS

I am not the one who hunts, the lioness does it

MY TONGUE IS
BLACK TO PROTECT
MYSELF FROM
SUNBURN

I DO NOT CHANGE COLOR TO CAMOUFLAGE MYSELF BUT TO EXPRESS MY MOOD AND EMOTIONS

Thank you so much for purchasing this book. If you enjoyed it, the please leave an Amazon review.

Reviews are the lifeblood of our publishing endeavors-leaving a positive review would mean the world to us.

Cheers!

- LuloSaurio Inc.

www.ingramcontent.com/pod-product-compliance
Lightning Source LLC
Chambersburg PA
CBHW081245250726
48654CB00012B/1491